IF YOU CAN DRAW THESE THINGS ⟶
YOU WILL BE ABLE TO DRAW
ALL THE THINGS IN THIS BOOK.

△ ∧ S ⌣
□ ⊓ . | ⌇⌇⌇
○ C D

FOR INSTANCE ——

THE BOTTOM ROW TELLS WHAT TO DRAW. THE TOP ROW TELLS WHERE TO PUT IT.

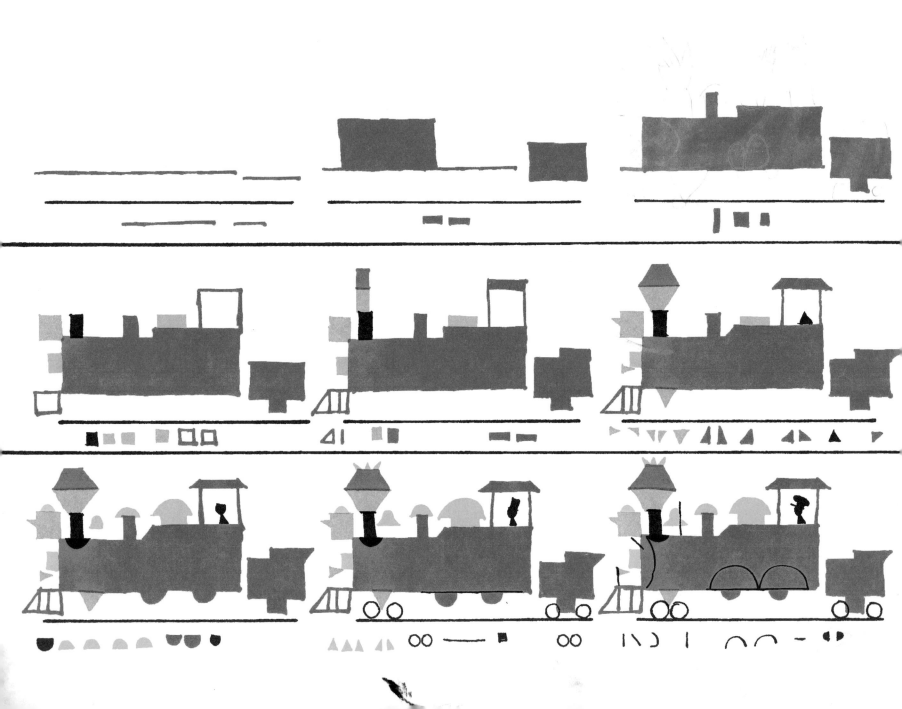

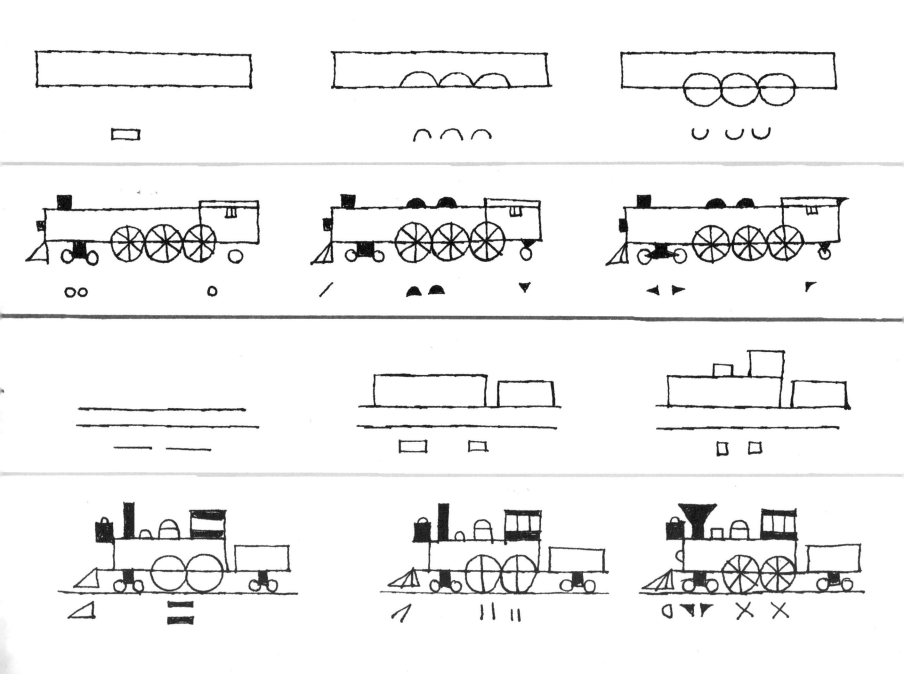

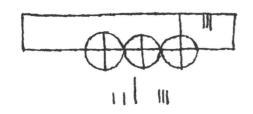
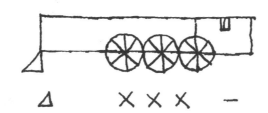
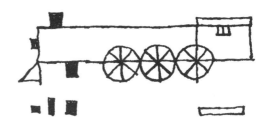

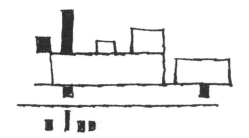

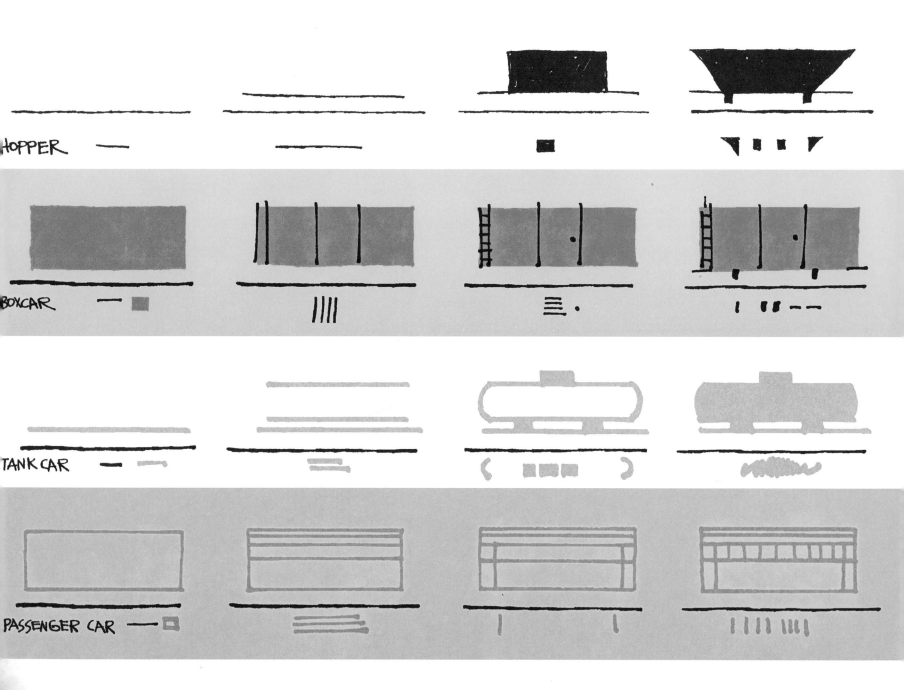

HOPPER

BOXCAR

TANK CAR

PASSENGER CAR

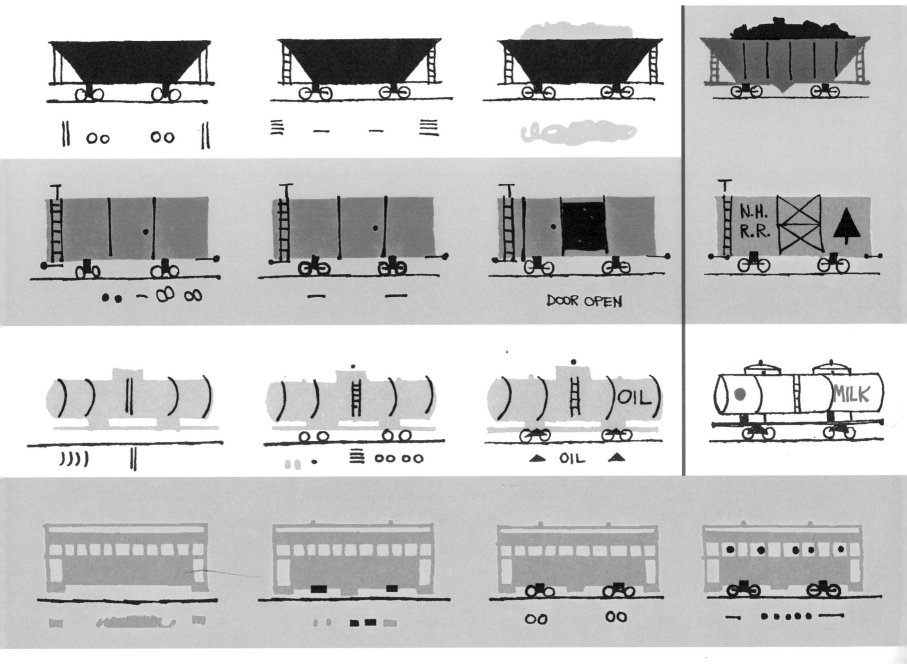

DOOR OPEN

N.H.
R.R.

)))) ||

OIL

MILK

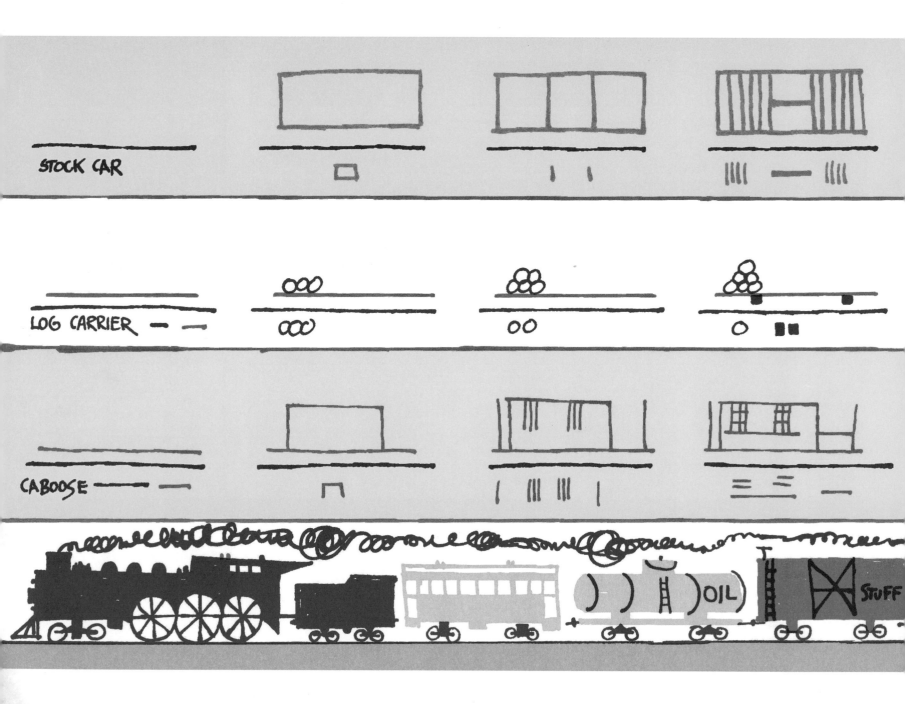

STOCK CAR

LOG CARRIER

CABOOSE

OIL

STUFF

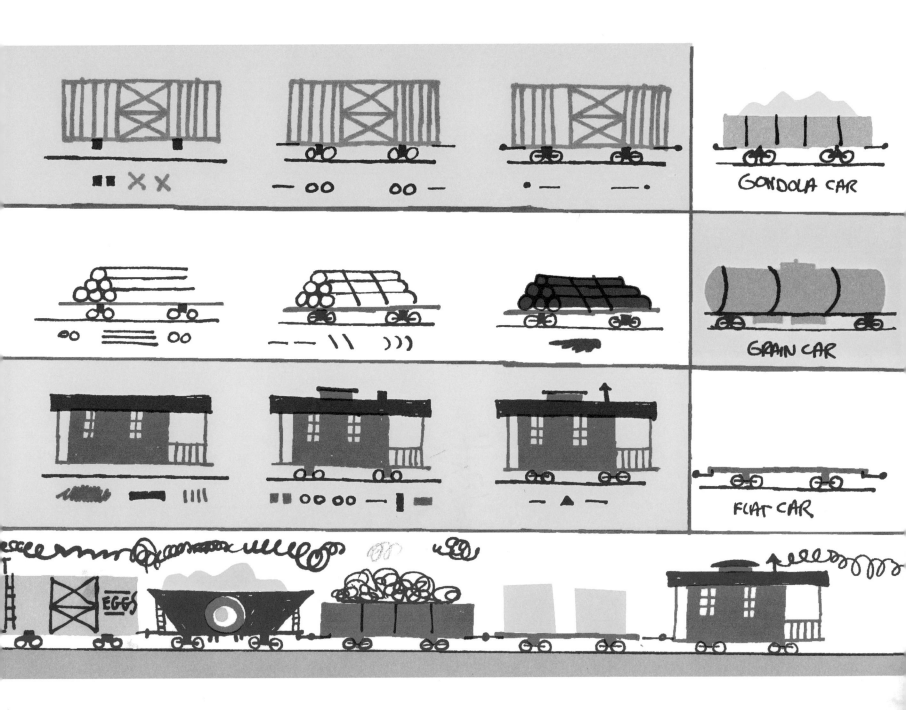

GONDOLA CAR

GRAIN CAR

FLAT CAR

EGGS

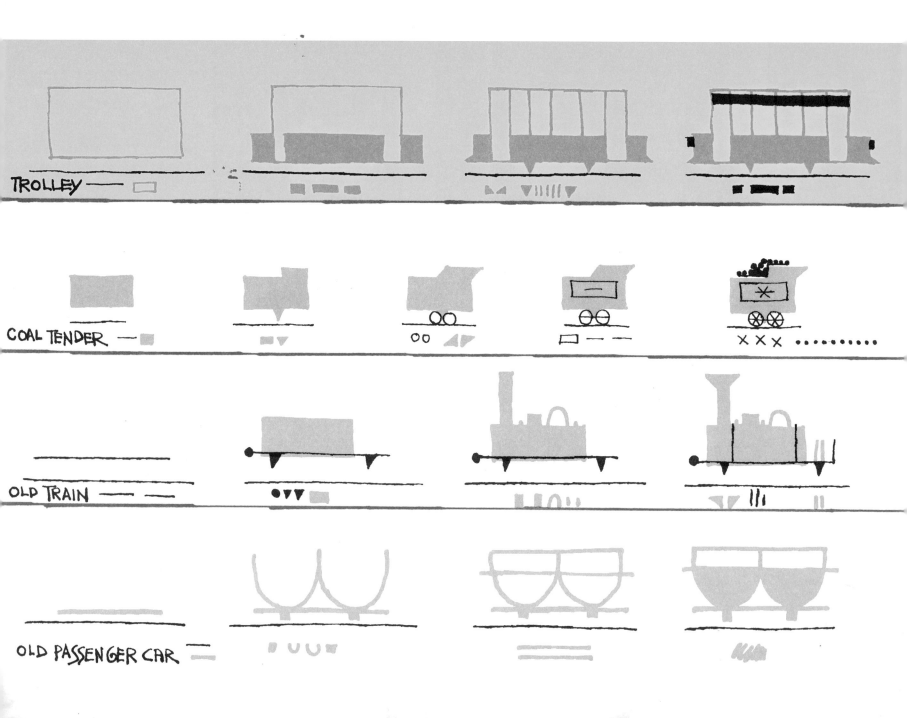

TROLLEY

COAL TENDER

OLD TRAIN

OLD PASSENGER CAR

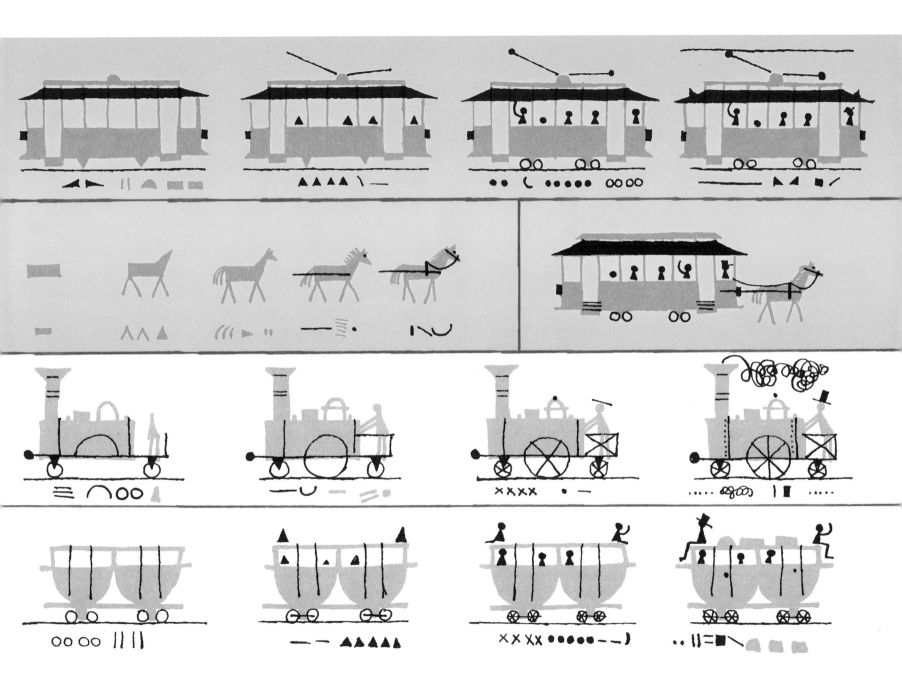

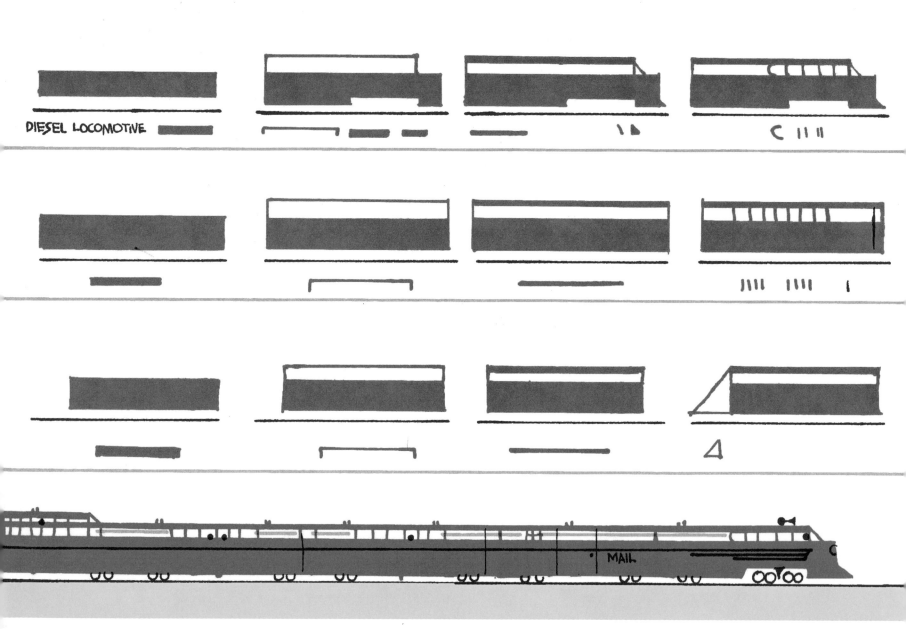

DIESEL LOCOMOTIVE

MAIL

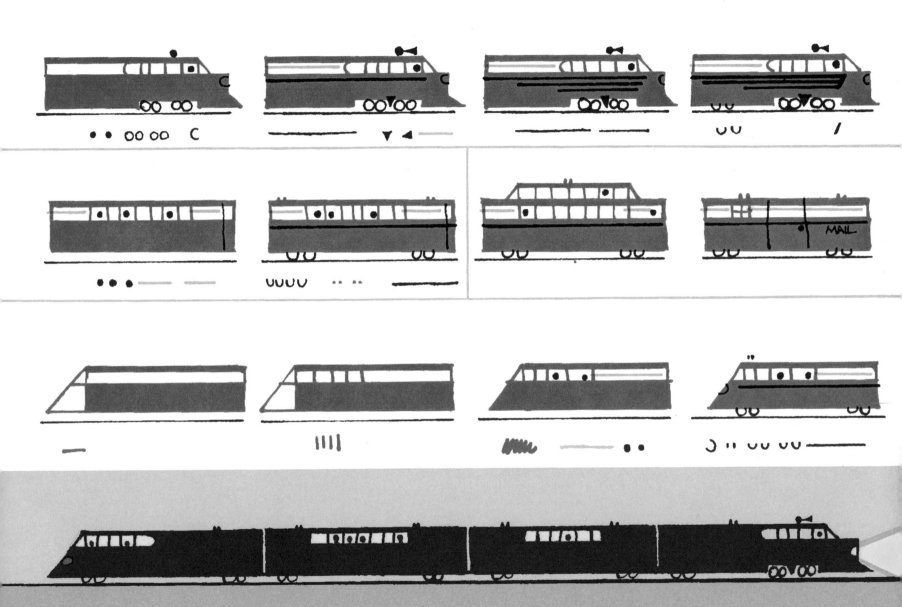

BAGGAGE CART

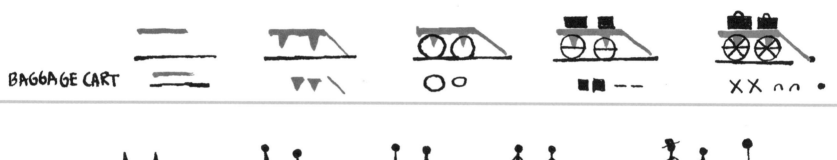

PASSENGERS

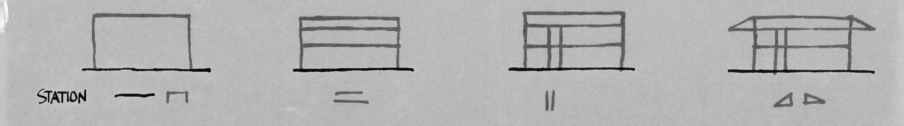

STATION

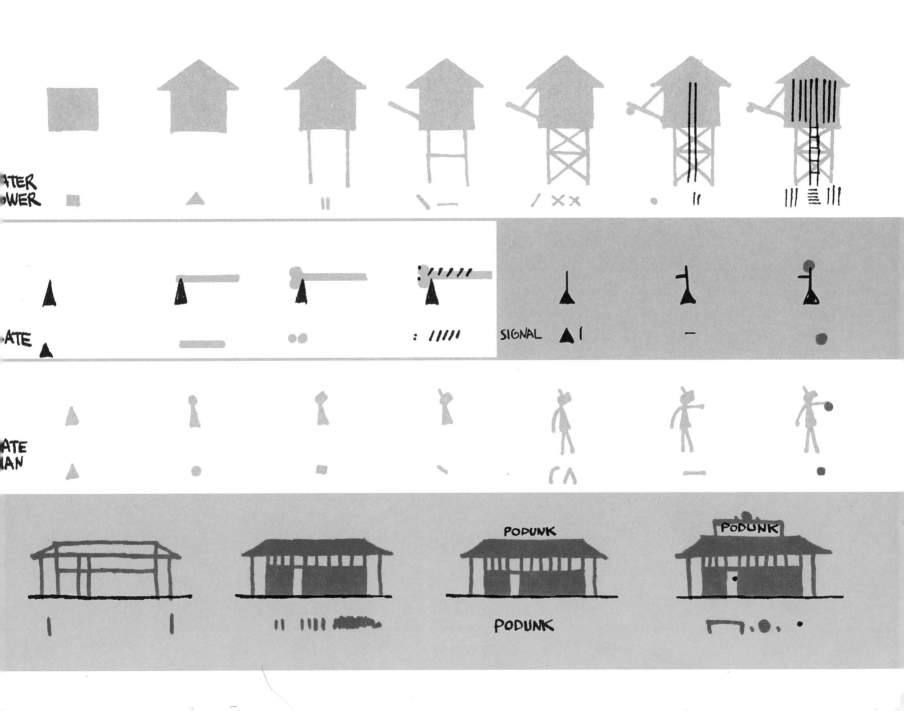

WATER TOWER

GATE

GATE MAN

SIGNAL

PODUNK

PODUNK

PODUNK

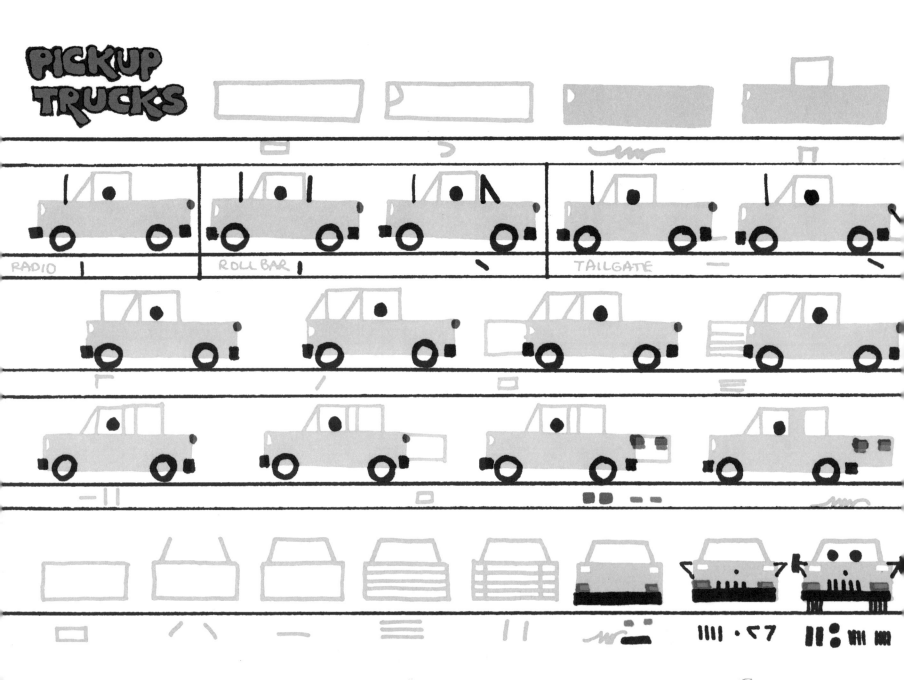

PICKUP TRUCKS

RADIO

ROLL BAR

TAILGATE

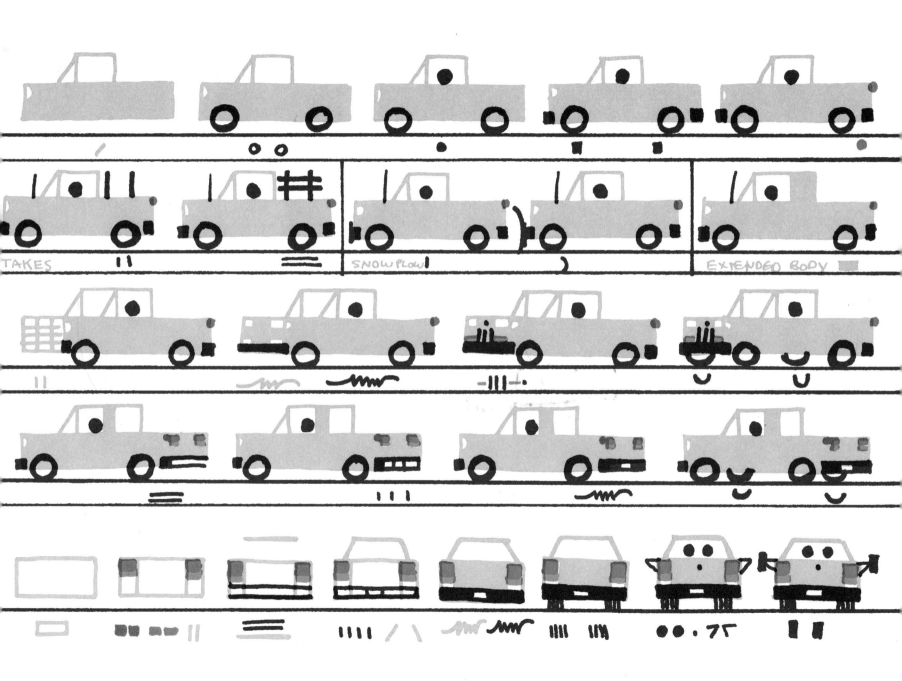

TAKES

SNOW PLOW

EXTENDED BODY

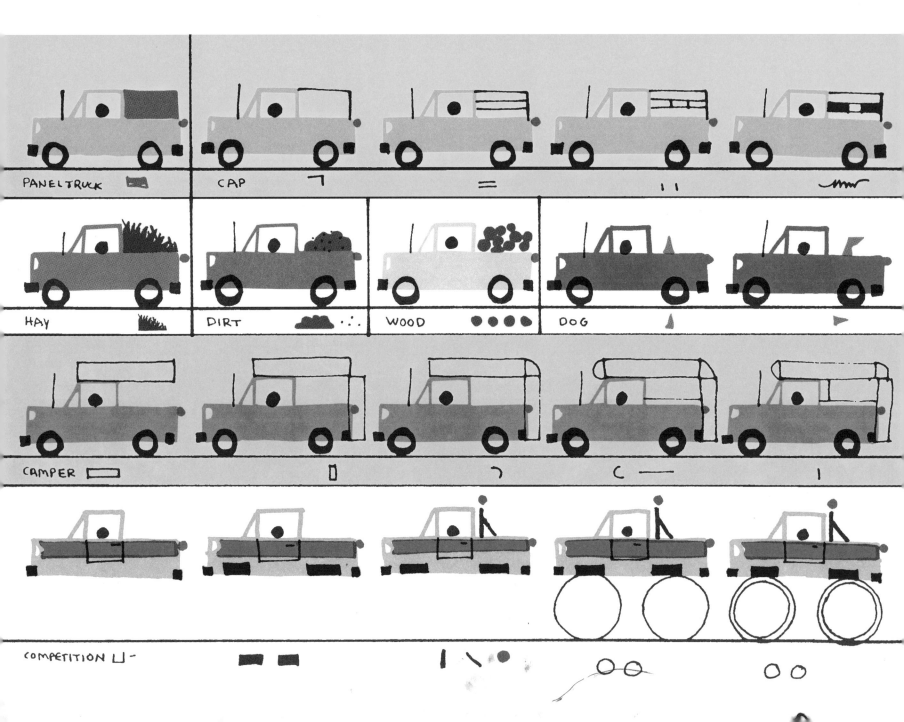

PANEL TRUCK   CAP   = ||

HAY   DIRT   WOOD ●●●●   DOG

CAMPER ▭   ▯   ⌐   C — |

COMPETITION ⊔—   ▬ ▬ | ＼●   ○○   ○○

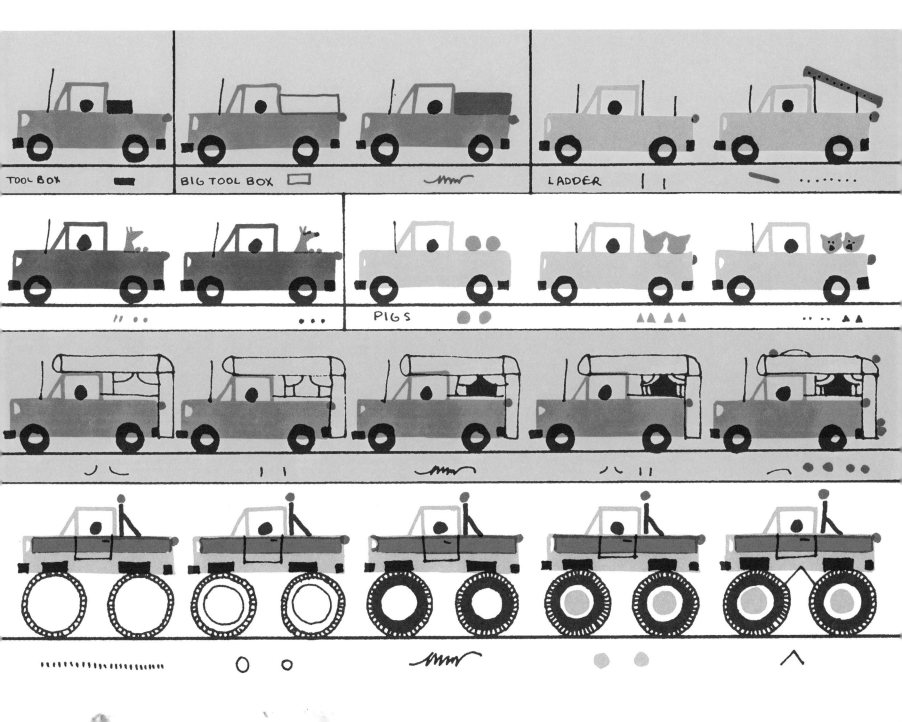

TOOL BOX

BIG TOOL BOX

LADDER

PIGS

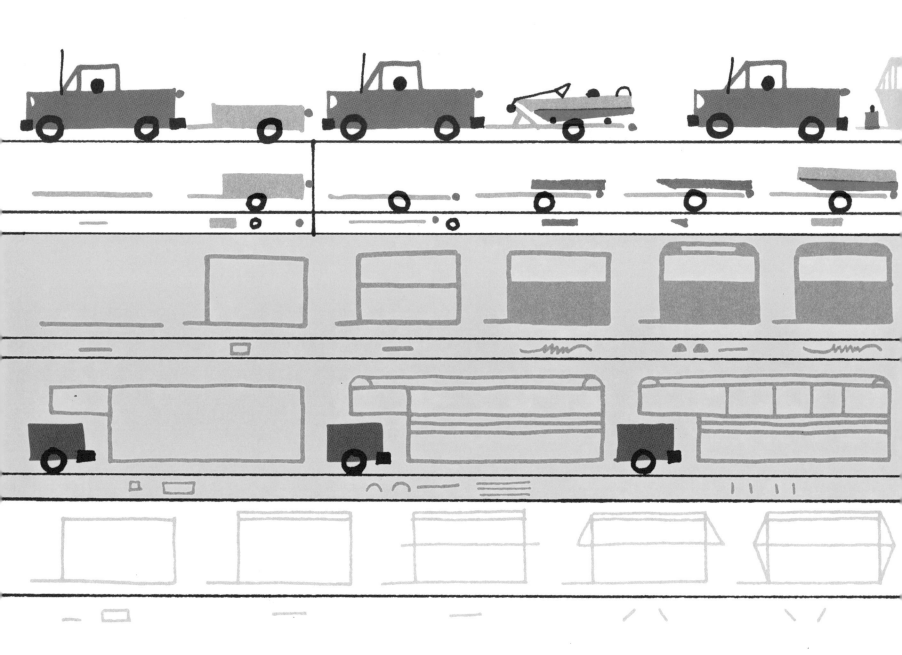

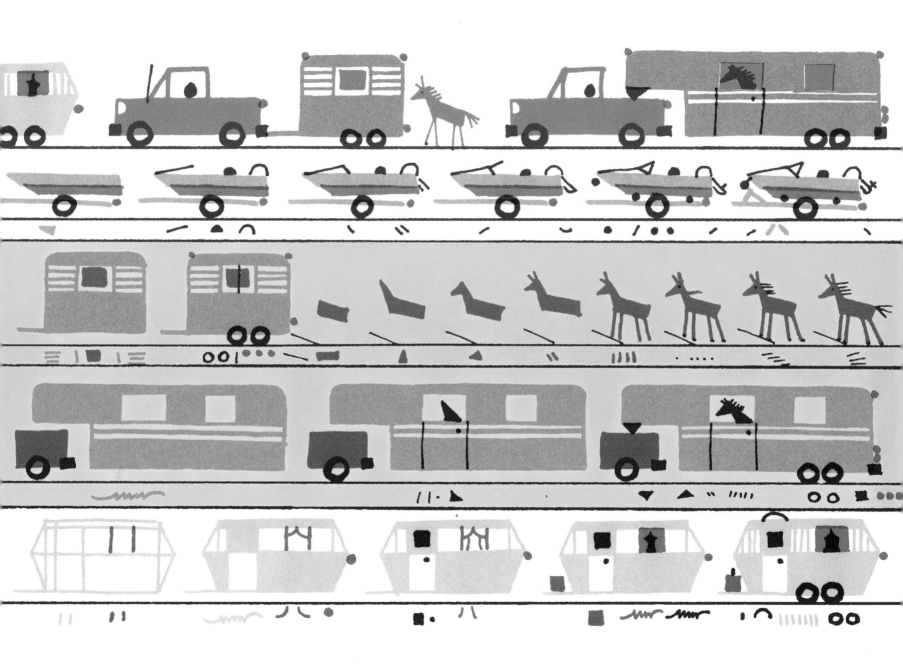

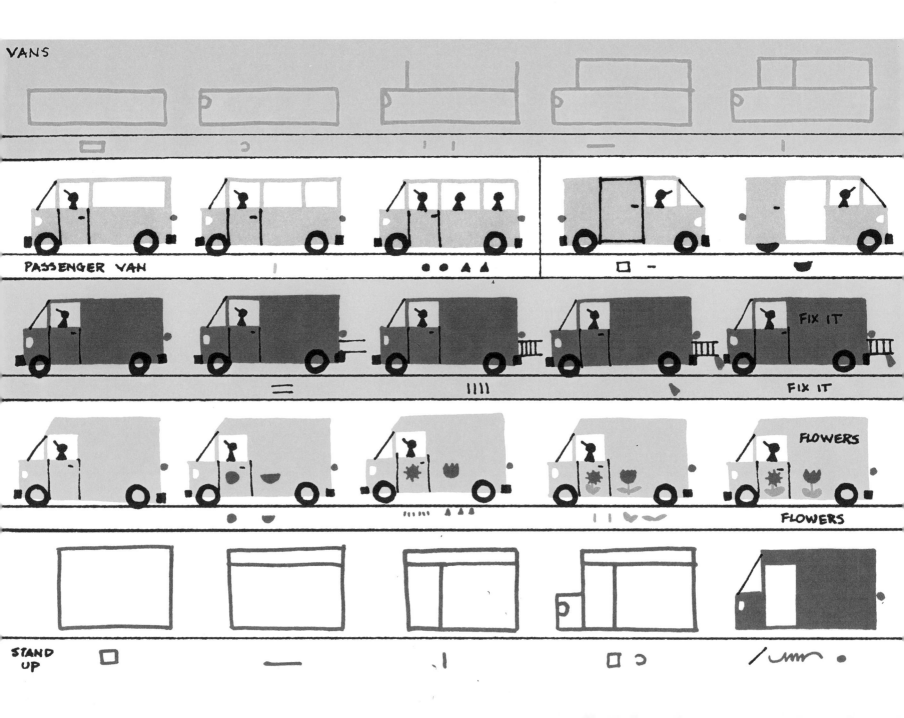

VANS

PASSENGER VAN

FIX IT

FLOWERS

STAND UP

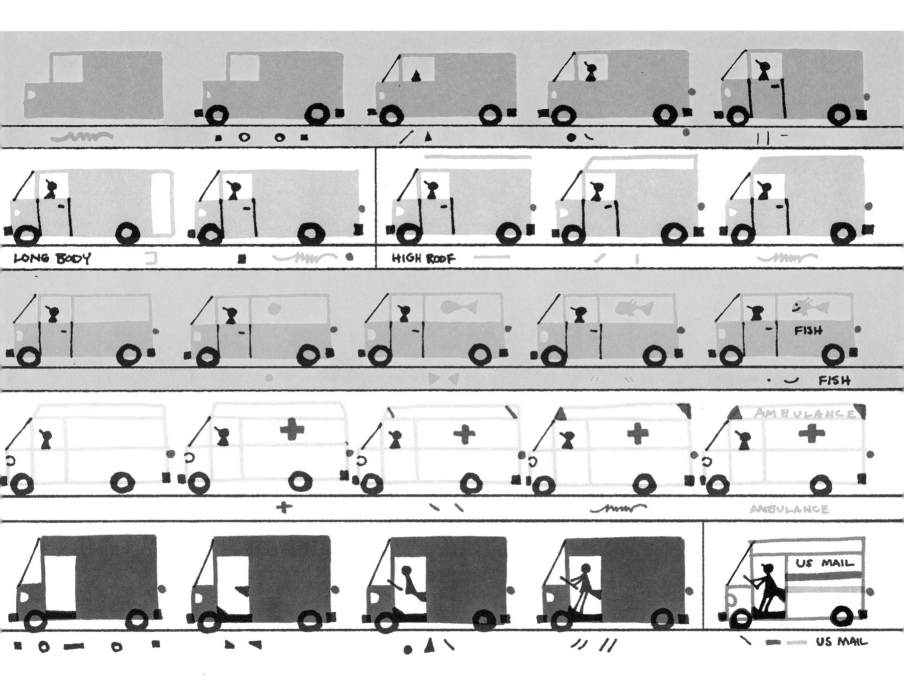

LONG BODY

HIGH ROOF

FISH

FISH

AMBULANCE

AMBULANCE

US MAIL

US MAIL

HEAVY TRUCKS

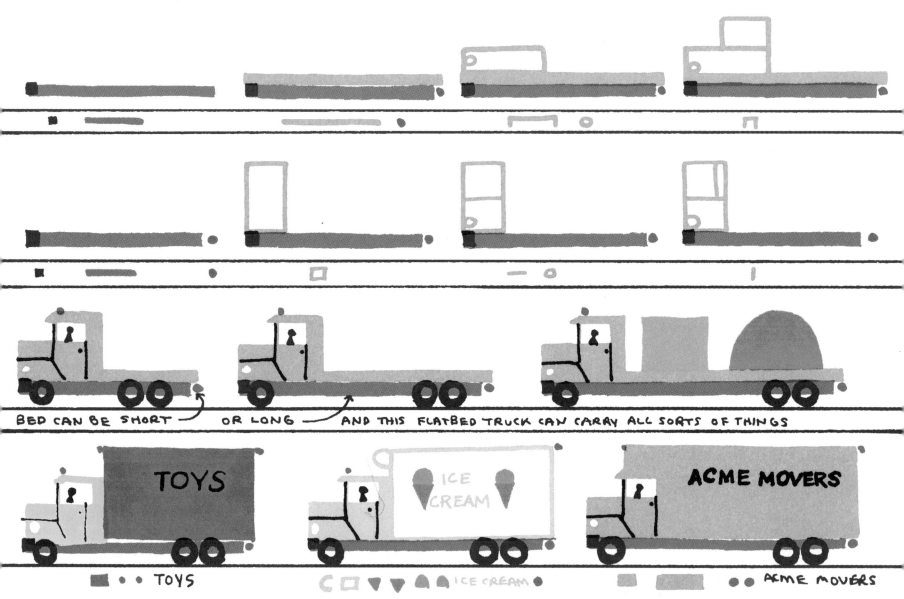

BED CAN BE SHORT — OR LONG — AND THIS FLATBED TRUCK CAN CARRY ALL SORTS OF THINGS

TOYS

ICE CREAM

ACME MOVERS

TOYS · · · TOYS

ICE CREAM

ACME MOVERS

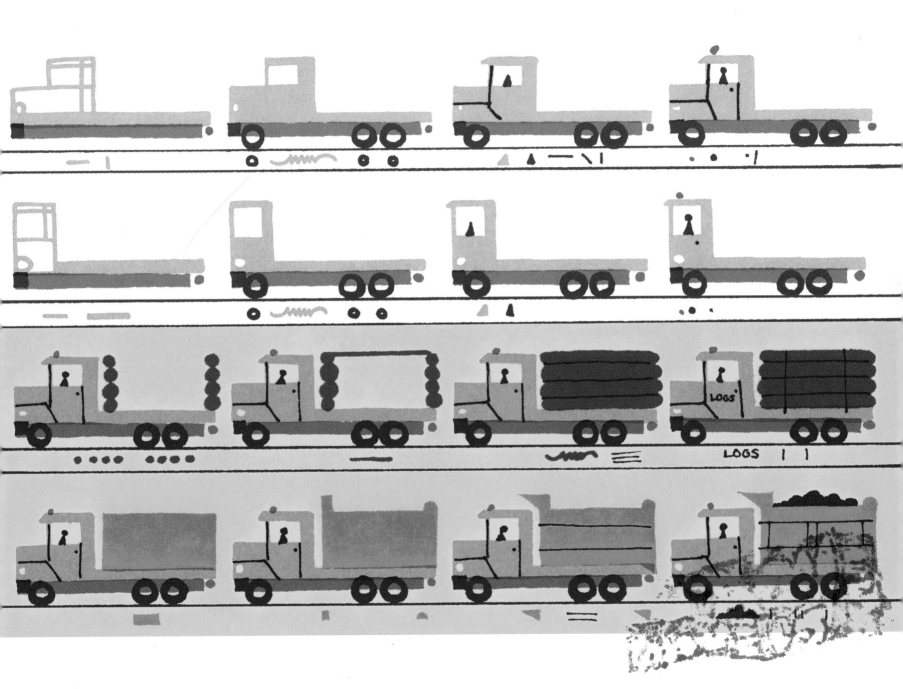

PROPANE

PROPANE

CEMENT

CEMENT

TRASH

TRASH

TOW

TOW

MILK

ADD TRUCK

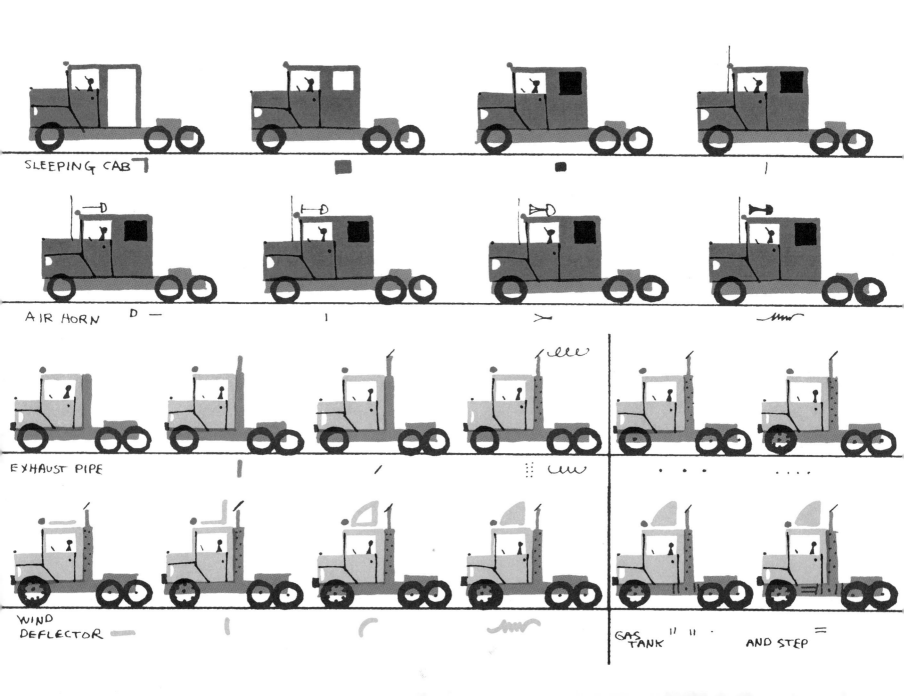

SLEEPING CAB

AIR HORN

EXHAUST PIPE

WIND
DEFLECTOR

GAS
TANK   AND STEP

First Edition

ISBN 0-316-23898-8 (hc) / ISBN 0-316-23786-8 (pb)
LCCN 2001041744

10 9 8 7 6 5 4 3 2

TWP

Printed in Singapore

FEB   2005